101 *Amazing* Things About God

by

Marsha Marks

RIVER OAK

PUBLISHING

Tulsa, Oklahoma

101 Amazing Things about God
ISBN 1-57919-980-4
Copyright © 2001 by Marsha Marks

Published by RiverOak Publishing
P.O. Box 700143
Tulsa, Oklahoma 74170-0143

DEDICATION

*I*t may seem odd that I would dedicate this book to an atheist, but if you could meet Hannah Gray, you'd understand. She is charming, witty, and funny; and she makes cerebral palsy seem like only a minor handicap.

I met Hannah when she was ten years old. She was traveling with her mom on a flight on which I was working as a flight attendant. It was a long flight, and we had time to talk. When she left, she gave me a note printed in pencil by a hand that shakes against her will. I've kept that note all these years. It says, "Dear flight attendant (Marsha), Thank you for being so nice to me. It was a pleasure to have someone to talk to. Love, Hannah Gray." Hannah invited me to e-mail her, and once, she told me she absolutely does not believe in God at all.

But you don't have to believe in God for me to love you. So I dedicate this book to my atheist friend, Hannah Gray.

ACKNOWLEDGMENTS

My thanks to Connie Smiley whom God provided to design the cover of the book, to Sealy Yates whom God provided to give me confidence, and to my husband, Tom Marks, whom God provided to show me His love.

INTRODUCTION

*I*f you were to ask several different people to describe me, you'd get a variety of answers. Some, such as the ones who were loud when I was trying to sleep, would say I'm cranky. Others, like my four-year-old daughter and her friends, would say I'm fun. Still others—my husband, at least—would say I'm loving, warm, and sweet. All of those answers would be true of me, at least from the perspective of the person asked.

That's what I think the Bible is like. Many people who knew God wrote about Him. Some saw in Him an aspect that was scary. Others saw Him as fun-loving. Some saw Him as one who takes action against infractions. But then there were those who saw Him as loving, warm, and sweeter than honey—in a word, amazing. That's how I see God, and the joy I have in seeing Him this way has bubbled over in the form of this book, *101 Amazing Things about God*.

Marsha Marks

1

HE LOVES HIS ENEMIES.

*God has enemies.
How does He respond
to them? Why, He lavishes
them with gifts, including
the One closest to His heart.*

*God so loved the world that he gave his
one and only Son, that whoever believes in
him shall not perish but have eternal life.*
—JOHN 3:16

2

HE SAVES ALL MY PRAYERS . . .

I save my daughter's hair and her pictures and paintings. God saves our prayers for the same reason— because He loves us.

They were holding golden bowls of incense, which are the prayers of the saints.
REVELATION 5:8

3

. . . AND USES THEM
AS THE FRAGRANCE
OF HEAVEN.

Remember a time when the

scent of something brought

back a wonderful memory?

So does God.

---

*Another angel, who had a golden censer, came
and stood at the altar. He was given much
incense to offer, with the prayers of all the
saints, on the golden altar before the throne.*

*The smoke of the incense, together with
the prayers of the saints, went up before God.*
REVELATION 8:3-4

4

HE GIVES A NEW BATCH OF MERCY EACH MORNING.

*M*ercy is the sponge He uses to clean us when we're dirty. Grace is the water He uses as a rinse. And, as far as a bathtub, He doesn't have one; He just cradles us in His arms.

His compassions never fail.
They are new every morning.
LAMENTATIONS 3:22-23

5

HE CRADLES MY HEAD IN HIS HANDS AND LIFTS IT.

*W*hen I was a teenage girl, I used to dream of a man who would one day come into my life and lift my head in both of his hands and kiss me. In a way, God is like that—lifting our faces toward His and causing our hearts to sing, offering to carry what is too heavy for us and giving us only what is light and easy.

Earthly love, I think, is just a taste of heavenly love.

---

*O LORD; you bestow glory on me
and lift up my head.*

PSALM 3:3

6

HE IS
TRUSTWORTHY . . .

*. . . more so than the
ground we stand on,
the bank we bank in,
the family we love.*

---

*Your words are trustworthy, and
you have promised these good things.*
2 SAMUEL 7:28

7

HE KEEPS ME AS THE APPLE OF HIS EYE . . .

. . . the center of
His heart, the focus
of His thoughts.

Keep me as the apple of your eye;
hide me in the shadow of your wings.
PSALM 17:8

8

HE WILL SHOW ME THE PATH OF LIFE.

This implies that
there is another path
we seem to find on our own.

There is a way that seems right to a man,
but in the end it leads to death.
PROVERBS 14:12

9

HE DELIGHTS IN DOING GREAT THINGS FOR HIS CHILDREN.

To Him, His children are so precious that He can't help but do great things for them.

---

*Your righteousness reaches to the skies,
O God, you who have done great things.
Who, O God, is like you?*

PSALM 71:19

10

HE IS A COMFORTER, FILLED WITH THE FINEST DOWN FROM ABOVE.

The Flood

There are times when you've gone too far—when there is no more grace, I thought the day I flooded our condo. It wasn't just the flood. It was the flood tied in with the conversation I'd had with my husband the night before.

My husband of two years—normally a quiet man—had talked for forty-five minutes straight. It seemed there was a behavior of mine that had to stop and stop immediately.

"Marsha," Tom said, "you've ruined every place we've ever lived in, and I'm tired of it."

"I think 'ruin' is too strong a word," I said.

"You don't call seventy-two nail holes in three walls of our first apartment 'ruining'?"

"No, I call it trying to hang fourteen large pictures."

"It took me four hours to patch all the holes."

"That's what security deposits are for."

"I have never forfeited a security deposit," said Tom, thinking that would impress me.

"Really?" I said, "That's odd. I've never gotten one back."

"And the second place we lived?" Tom said, "Where you ruined the garage?"

"I didn't *ruin* it; I tried to remodel it."

"I had to hire a professional carpenter and pay him a huge amount of money to fix your remodel," said Tom. "I had asked you specifically not to ruin that place."

"That's why I stayed in the garage! You said, specifically, don't ruin this home! You didn't say I couldn't work in the garage."

"You weren't working," Tom said.

"I was," I said. "I have a secret desire to be a carpenter, and I was trying out my craft."

"You are not a carpenter. It takes years to become a skilled carpenter."

"I was practicing," I said.

"Well, I don't want you practicing on our homes, *or* our garages," he said.

"I was trying to save us money," I said.

Tom ignored my last comment and went on with his diatribe, "All this wouldn't have been so bad, except we've only been in this new condo for a day, and already you are starting to ruin it.

"I'm not!" I said.

"The closet!" he said.

"Oh! Well, I was trying out my new electric tools. I wanted to reorganize the shelves and racks and . . ."

"I hung my coat tonight, Marsha, on the rack you reorganized, and the entire thing fell to the floor *with* all my shirts and suits on it."

"I know," I said. "I don't know how to find those places that make things stick to the wall.

And I want you to know, it was only because I was so upset by what happened in the closet that I went into the kitchen in hopes of redeeming myself as a carpenter."

My husband shook his head; he'd already seen the kitchen.

"I know," he said, "and now you've ruined the kitchen too."

"No one will ever see if you keep that pantry door shut."

"Marsha, that pantry door is the first one people naturally open. Look," he said, opening the door in question. "See this shelf?"

I saw it. It was the one where my new SawsAll 850 Power Plus had gotten away from me.

"See this shelf," Tom said, apparently more irritated now that we were both looking at the damage. "IT'S NOT FIXABLE. It looks like a shark took a bite out of it."

"It was the SawsAll 850 Power Plus," I said. "I couldn't hold on to it." And then in a quiet voice I said, "It says saws *all*. It doesn't say it saws pretty."

"Listen," Tom said, taking a deep breath like he was going diving. "Listen," he said again, "I'm tired of this. We are now living in the nicest place we've ever lived, and I don't want you to ruin it—ANYMORE. I'm telling you now, you are not a carpenter. And I don't want you trying to become one by practicing on our places—not on our homes, not our garages, not our closets, not our kitchens, not even our pantries. You don't have the skill to be using power tools around the house. I don't want you to remodel anything. I don't even want you to walk though the Sears tool department without me there to keep you from buying something. Do you understand? You are outa control here, and it's ruining our home. Are you listening to me?"

I was listening, and despite the fact that my husband was overreacting, I said, "Okay, can we just go to sleep now?"

We did not sleep well that night. My husband's head was filled with nightmares of how I was ruining any real estate he'd saved to buy. And mine was filled with nightmares from my childhood during which my mother had been married five times and divorced four times. As each marriage had dissolved, she'd

said, "I just can't take this. I w
marriage where I'm unhappy."

I was thinking of how I'd made m
unhappy and how I knew from f
experience that people can only take so
and then they leave. By morning, I had ma
serious commitment to honor my precio
husband's request, unreasonable though i
seemed to me.

I could do it. I could just resist the temptation
to remodel this place anymore. In the rest of my
husband's lecture, he'd said he'd hire a
professional if I needed anything remodeled. I
love my husband and hated to see him upset. I
resolved I absolutely wasn't going to do
anything more to trash or injure this new place
he loved so much.

Tom went to work the next day, the second
full day in our new condo. After he left, the
builders knocked on my door and said, "We're
here to do a final inspection on your condo. We
know you just moved in, and we haven't
checked the whirlpool bath in the master
bathroom. Could you go up and turn on the

n check the jets
pperly?"

ld need to sit
with water,
nd it would
ub, and it

on't stay in a
husband
rsthand
much,
de a
us

ve were so newly in
nly phone we had hooked
stairs in the kitchen, so I ran
airs, fully intending to only be gone a
minute. But on the phone was my girlfriend, a fellow flight attendant who had just been in an auto accident.

It was a fascinating story. She'd been on a layover and was going back to the airport the next day when her van was hit broadside, and her neck was broken. She wasn't paralyzed or anything, but she was in the hospital and was giving me all the details. And I was, like any good friend, totally concentrating on everything she said—until I heard the strangest sound coming from my living room. It sounded like water splashing on the tiles around our fireplace. *How odd.* I ignored it for a minute. It was such a foreign sound, like a fountain bubbling in our living room.

But then it got louder, so I walked to the kitchen door. Glancing into the living room, I saw water pouring out of the recessed lights above the fireplace, cascading down our stairwell as if it were truly a place where a waterfall should be. I screamed to my friend, "I've flooded the place, I've got to go." And then I hung up the phone and swam upstream to the upstairs hall, through the master bedroom, over to the recessed floor in the bathroom, and to the tub to shut it off—knowing my marriage was over, knowing I was doomed. There's only so much a person can stand.

I wanted to run away. I didn't want to have to tell my husband, "Hey, Tom, you know the holes in the wall? Well, that's nothing!" I didn't want to hear him say, "That's it. Get out of my sight." I didn't want to face the horror of being asked to leave. I wanted to run on my own.

But now the builder was in our home, ripping up our brand-new, drenched carpet and knocking holes in our ceiling to get all the water out. He was screaming for his workmen to bring buckets and was yelling for me to get my insurance people out here now. "Call your husband," he said.

"Oh," I said, "I don't think so. I can't, really."

"You'd better get him on the phone now. We need some answers here."

And so—on what I'd come to accept as the last day of my married life—with trembling hands, I dialed my husband. The phone rang in his office, and his secretary told me he was in a meeting. "Well, you need to get him out. This is important."

Tom came to the phone. In the background of our home there was pandemonium. I started to cry. I couldn't talk, I was crying so hard.

"What's wrong?" Tom said.

"I can't tell you," I said.

"What's wrong, honey?" he said.

I thought, *O sure you're saying* honey *now, but wait till you hear.* "I can't tell you," I said.

"Marsha," he said, "I'm in a meeting. What's wrong?"

The men in the background were getting louder—shouting to each other to bring buckets and starting up the ShopVac.

"What's that noise?" Tom asked.

"Oh, just, um—honey—I flooded the place," I said, then started to cry again.

"What?" said Tom, "I didn't hear you correctly. What?"

"I flooded the place," I said.

"What do you mean?" he said.

"I mean I flooded the place." And then I told him the whole story, starting with the builders and ending with the fact that they were now tearing up all our carpet to hang it over the balcony to dry.

Tom paused for a long time and then quietly said, "Do you need me to come home and comfort you?"

Now it was my turn to be in shock.

"What?" I said.

"Do you need me to come home and comfort you? Are you gonna be okay?"

Do you need me to come home and comfort you?
Do you need me to come home and comfort you?

In that moment I learned the shocking truth of grace. Grace is what we give to those who have just trashed what we value.

When my husband came home that evening, he took me in his arms and told me how much he loved me and cared for me. I told him that his reaction that day had taught me about God's love for me.

It's been twelve years since the night I flooded our condo; and every time I tell this story, people are amazed at the grace my husband offered.

Because of Tom's response, I now understand how God responds to my blunders—with a comfort filled with the finest down from above. I also understand what it means for husbands to love their wives as Christ loves the Church.

Praise be to . . . the Father of
compassion and the God of all comfort,
who comforts us in all our troubles, so that
we can comfort those in any trouble with the
comfort we ourselves have received from God.
2 CORINTHIANS 1:3-4

11

HE IS WITH ME
NO MATTER
WHERE I GO.

But sometimes my heart

has to turn to see Him.

The LORD your God will be with you
wherever you go.

JOSHUA 1:9

12

HE DOES NOT WANT ME TO BE AFRAID OR DISCOURAGED.

*W*hen I am afraid, I will run away; and when I am discouraged, I will look around me or down at my feet.

He wants me to be still and look up to Him.

Do not be afraid or discouraged.
JOSHUA 1:9 NLT

13

HE DID NOT SEND
HIS SON INTO THE
WORLD TO CONDEMN
THE WORLD.

And He didn't send

me into the world to

condemn the world either.

---

*God did not send his Son into the
world to condemn the world, but to
save the world through him.*

JOHN 3:17

14

THE HEAVENS ARE THE WORK OF HIS FINGERS.

*H*is fingers—the vast heavens. We're not talking the work of His hands, just His fingers. As if He were working with clay, He shaped the vastness of space.

When I consider your heavens, the work of your fingers, the moon and the stars, which you have set in place, what is man that you are mindful of him, the son of man that you care for him?
PSALM 8:3-4

15

HE ENTRUSTS ALL HIS CREATION TO MAN.

I have known a lot of artists, but I have never known one to entrust his work to someone who doesn't appreciate its value. But God does. He entrusts the work of His hands to people who are His enemies. What kind of God is this?

What is man that you are mindful of him? . . .
You made him ruler over the works of your hands.
PSALM 8:4,6

16

THERE IS NOTHING ANYONE CAN DO TO YOU THAT GOD CANNOT USE FOR HIS GLORY.

*W*hen God needed someone to do a very important task, He chose Moses, a man who had been put up for adoption, was exiled from his adoptive family, and was forced to leave the country for years.

To bestow on them a crown of beauty instead of ashes. . . . They will be called . . . a planting of the LORD for the display of his splendor.
ISAIAH 61:3

17

HE HEARS ME
WHEN I WEEP.

*M*y four-year-old can wail. When she doesn't get what she wants, she can really cry her heart out. It's short lived. But I have to tell you, I hear her when she weeps. And sometimes, all I'm able to offer is myself.

The LORD has heard my weeping.
The LORD has heard my cry.

PSALM 6:8-9

18

HE GIVES ME GLORY.

*T*he moon has no light of its own. All its light comes from the sun. In the same way, God designed people so that when they live with their faces turned toward Him, their lives will glow—and glow they do, much to the chagrin of those who prefer the dark.

O LORD; you bestow glory on me.

PSALM 3:3

19

HE PRODUCES LIFE OUT OF DEATH.

*W*hen my daughter was three years old, she told me that Christmas trees have to be cut down so they can have a Christmas. "Only the ones that get cut down get to have Christmas," she said.

In a way, that's what God says to us. Only when we give Him all we are do we experience all He is—the miracle of Christmas.

What you sow does not come to life unless it dies.

1 CORINTHIANS 15:36

20

ALL GOOD GIFTS COME FROM HIM.

If it's good,

it's from God.

Every good and perfect gift is from above.

JAMES 1:17

21

HE CAN
BRING PEASANTS
BEFORE KINGS.

The King and the Middle-aged Lady

When I get to Heaven, I want to meet Queen Esther, because she also made an appointment to meet a king—after she'd prayed, of course.

*S*ometimes prayer is the only connection you may ever have with some people.

I was thinking about this as I read the book *Another Life: A Memoir of Other People* and began praying for its author, Michael Korda.

I prayed for his spiritual well-being for a full day before I got the idea to pray that I could meet him. Meeting him had seemed so out of the question. He was, after all, a world-famous author who had been the editor in chief at Simon and Schuster for thirty years and had a movie-star mother and a family who hobnobbed with European royalty. I was a middle-aged housewife whose only glamour was going to work as a flight attendant. The closest I'd been to a movie star was when one sat in first class and wrapped a blanket around his head.

I saw Mr. Korda as an East Coast king; and I, pretty much, was a West Coast peasant.

But his book *Another Life: A Memoir of Other People* inspired and encouraged me with its accounts of the publishing careers of all the writers I'd grown up hearing about. It made me realize that struggling to get recognized is a part of most famous people's careers.

I decided that someday, when I was old, I would love the chance to meet Mr. Korda and tell him how much his book had meant to me.

So, in addition to praying for his spiritual welfare, I began to pray, as Esther prayed, that one day God would arrange a meeting with a king.

I thought about giving God some suggestions. *I'm a flight attendant,* I reasoned. *I could meet Mr. Korda while he is traveling first class.*

Then an idea came to me. Why didn't I just call up Michael Korda? It was such a radical thing. But the idea was that as a flight attendant, I sometimes have layovers in New York; maybe I could just stop by his office and meet with him for five minutes. It could happen. So I prayed that if this was a good idea for me, God would make it happen. I knew the book of Esther; God can bring peasants before kings. I knew Proverbs 21:1; He can turn the king's heart.

I kept praying, and then I acted on my prayer. I picked up the phone and dialed New York. I got the number for Simon and Schuster Publishing, and when the receptionist answered the phone, I asked if a Michael Korda still worked there. Boom. Transferred. "Hello, this is Mr. Korda's office." I must have reached his assistant.

And then, I am sorry to tell you, I went nuts. This sometimes happens to me when I get too excited. I just go nuts. I started screaming. "Mr. Korda's office! I can't believe it! I love him! I just love him! I have to meet him! Where is he?"

"Well, he's currently on tour with his new book, *Another Life*."

"YES!" I screamed a lot louder than I should have, and I didn't shut up.

I don't really want to relive the whole awful conversation I had with Mr. Korda's assistant that day. Suffice it to say, when you call a major literary figure and you start screaming and saying you have to meet him and you begin demanding to know where he is, people get nervous. I'm pretty sure they patched me into security just before they hung up on me.

So I got off the phone and told God, "Well, that didn't work. I tried and failed."

Then I got this other idea. I'd try again. Only this time I'd act more subdued. And this time, the idea was to call his publisher. I'd call his publisher and ask them if they minded if I wrote a review on his book. I hadn't even realized that although Mr. Korda worked at Simon and Schuster, his publisher for *Another Life* was Random House.

So again, I prayed, *God if this is something that is good for me to do, You will work it out.* Then I called Random House in New York and asked to speak to the editor of Michael Korda's book *Another Life*. These New York receptionists were savvy.

"Why do you want to speak to that editor?"

I had already thought of a rational answer, should that question come up. "Well, I want to write a review for his book."

Boom. Transferred to the publicity department.

"Publicity department, Random House."

This was getting exciting, but I remained calm. "Hello, I've just read Michael Korda's new book, *Another Life*, and I want to write a favorable review on it."

"Where do you live?"

I thought that was an odd question, but I answered it, "On the West Coast."

"You'll need West Coast publicity. Here is their number."

I called West Coast publicity and told them I wanted to write a review on Michael Korda's book *Another Life*.

"For what publication?"

Oh no! I hadn't thought *that* far in advance. I looked down at the kitchen counter and saw a magazine called *Writer's Digest*. "For *Writer's Digest* magazine," I said. (I didn't mention I was writing the review on spec.)

"Oh," said the publicity manager, "can I call you right back? I'm in a meeting."

"Sure," I said and gave her my number.

When I got off the phone, I immediately got another call from a friend of mine who had actually written for *Writer's Digest*. I hadn't heard from her in months, and I was quite excited to tell her the story that had just transpired.

"Are you NUTS?" she said. "You can't just tell publicity for Random House that you are writing an article for *Writer's Digest* magazine without telling *Writer's Digest* magazine. What if they call *Writer's Digest* and they say they've never heard of you? ARE YOU NUTS?" she said again.

People ask me if I'm nuts quite often, so I let that slide. "Okay," I said, "you've made your point. I will just call *Writer's Digest* magazine and tell them the whole story.

But before I could call *Writer's Digest* magazine and tell them what I'd done, the publicity department for Random House called back.

"Okay, now where did you say you lived? Just outside Seattle? Well, today is Tuesday. Mr. Korda is going to be in Seattle on Thursday, day after tomorrow. He is doing *Entertainment Weekly* at eleven and *Amazon.com* after that, but he could see you for twenty minutes at one. How does your schedule look on Thursday?"

I looked at my then two-year-old playing peacefully on the floor, then at my bare calendar and said, "Thursday at one is good." Then I said, "This isn't a book signing, is it?" I just couldn't believe I was going to meet Michael Korda alone for twenty minutes, forty-eight hours after I'd prayed to meet him.

"No," the publicity lady said. "This is a private meeting, but you only have twenty minutes. Okay?"

I said okay and put down the phone and started laughing and dancing a jig around the pans my daughter was playing with on our kitchen floor.

Then I called *Writer's Digest* magazine. I got an editor there who listened to my confession and assured me that if asked, he would at least say he had talked to me; and, yes, they were aware I would be meeting with Mr. Korda and writing an article on spec.

Ten minutes later my phone rang again. A serious-voiced woman identified herself as the managing editor of *Writer's Digest* magazine. "Marsha Marks?"

"Yes."

"I understand you are meeting with Michael Korda."

"Yes."

"Well *Writer's Digest* was wondering if you would accept an assignment from us. We'll pay you (serious money) to ask Mr. Korda several questions from us. If you agree, I will e-mail the questions and our contract to you so you can review them before you meet with Mr. Korda. And we'd like to rush this interview into our August edition."

I did not think it was necessary to tell this managing editor I had never interviewed anyone in my life. Instead I told her, "Yes, I will accept the assignment."

Then I called back the publicity people at Random House and told them that the managing editor at *Writer's Digest* had just called with quite a few questions they were planning to use in a rush article for their August edition. So the publicity person said, "Well, you're going to need more time then, so we'll give you one hour."

And that is how I, a middle-aged lady who read a book and prayed a prayer, got to interview a king in the publishing industry (after I bought a tape recorder of course). And that is how I got my first major assignment with a major magazine.

God can do anything.

If you'd like to read another story about a woman who made an appointment to see a king, read the book of Esther in the Bible.

The king's heart is in the hand of the LORD,
Like the rivers of water;
He turns it wherever He wishes.
PROVERBS 21:1 NKJV

22

THE ARROGANT CANNOT STAND IN HIS PRESENCE.

*H*ave you ever been so stunned by something that you took a few steps back and then almost fell over? That's how it will be one day when the arrogant are brought before God. They will be knocked to their knees by His awesomeness.

The arrogant cannot stand in your presence.
PSALM 5:5

23

HE SENT
AN ENGRAVED
INVITATION FOR
US TO COME BEFORE
HIS THRONE AND
RECEIVE HELP.

The engraving is on

the palms of Jesus.

---

*Let us then approach the throne of
grace with confidence.*

HEBREWS 4:16

24

HE CAN MAKE THE STAIN OF SIN DISAPPEAR.

I don't know if you've ever felt the stain of doing something wrong, of knowing you have offended the God who keeps accounts of such things, but knowing it's been blotted out by Him who holds you accountable is a wonderful thing.

"Come now, let us reason together," says the LORD.

"Though your sins are like scarlet, they shall be as white as snow; though they are red as crimson, they shall be like wool."
ISAIAH 1:18

HE HAS WRITTEN A BOOK, WATCHED OVER ITS PUBLICATION AND DISTRIBUTION, AND MADE SURE IT NEVER GOES OUT OF PRINT.

*T*here are over 156,000 books published each year. Most of them are on the shelves less than fifty-two days. How did a book that was written before there were printing presses remain in print all these years and remain a best-seller? Its author must rely on word-of-mouth advertising.

All Scripture is God-breathed.

2 TIMOTHY 3:16

26

HE ONCE PROMISED PARADISE TO A CRIMINAL IN THE MIDST OF AN EXECUTION.

I love this story because it tells us that as long as we have at least one breath in our bodies, a turn to Christ will be met with His acceptance. He embraces those who embrace Him.

Then [one of the criminals being executed with Jesus] said, "Jesus, remember me when you come into your kingdom." Jesus answered him, "I tell you the truth, today you will be with me in paradise."

LUKE 23:42-43

27

HE STOOPS DOWN
TO MAKE ME GREAT.

*T*he God of the universe stoops down to make His creation great. The God of the universe communicates with us through the written Word and invites us to communicate with Him. The God of the universe cares about my problems and my future. He stoops down for me; no wonder they call Him Father.

You stoop down to make me great.

PSALM 18:35

28

HE THINKS ABOUT
ME ALL THE TIME.

*G*od compares His thoughts about us to the grains of sand at the sea. That's how numerous they are. As for how tender they are, He uses the mental picture of a loving parent with a child. I didn't understand this parent/child illustration until I had my daughter. Then I began to realize the thickness of parent/child love—how it gets into your brain and expands it with thoughts of the one you love.

How precious to me are your thoughts,
O God! How vast is the sum of them!
Were I to count them, they would outnumber
the grains of sand.
When I awake, I am still with you.
PSALM 139:17-18

29

HE REVEALS HIS SECRETS TO ME.

When I was a little girl, I felt privileged to know the secrets of my best friend. It's not different now that I'm older.

The knowledge of the secrets of the kingdom of heaven has been given to you.

MATTHEW 13:11

30

HIS EYES SEE IN THE DARK WITH PERFECT CLARITY.

How wonderful for

those who want to do good,

and how terrible for those

who want to do evil.

Where can I go from your Spirit? Where can I flee from your presence? . . . If I say, "Surely the darkness will hide me . . . even the darkness will not be dark to you; the night will shine like the day, for darkness is as light to you.
PSALM 139:7,11-12

31

HE IS AN INTERIOR DECORATOR.

On the Door of Our New Home

Before you look inside this home
you need to know
the occupant isn't finished decorating, so . . .

There are some rooms that show what's mine
but most will be redone in time.

For example, in the room to the right,
you may see . . .
nothing in it came from me.

And rooms in the middle
contain older things
that really need recovering.

But one day, you'll be able to detect
who we are by what our home reflects.

Until then, we invite you in,
with the thought,

Could it be,
God wants to pin this same warning on me?

The fruit of the Spirit is love, joy,
peace, patience, kindness, goodness,
faithfulness, gentleness and self-control.
GALATIANS 5:22-23

32

HE REWARDS THOSE WHO DILIGENTLY SEEK HIM.

*T*he odd thing about God's giving rewards is how important it is to Him that we believe He will reward us. He says we cannot please Him if we don't believe it. But I suppose the idea of His wanting us to think the best of Him isn't odd when I think of my daughter in relation to me.

If Mandy chose to believe I was not incredibly concerned with helping her find the very best she can get out of life, it would break my heart. And I don't have a fraction of the resources for reward that God does—nor, I suppose, a fraction of His capacity to love.

Without faith it is impossible to please Him,
for he who comes to God must believe
that He is, and that He is a rewarder
of those who diligently seek Him.
HEBREWS 11:6 NKJV

33

HE SET THE HEAVENS
IN PLACE AND LAID
THE FOUNDATIONS
OF THE EARTH.

He may have used time,
movement, winds, and
floods to do it all; but
He did it nonetheless.

My own hand laid the foundations of the earth,
and my right hand spread out the heavens.
ISAIAH 48:13

34

HE REVEALS HIS
THOUGHTS TO ME.

I reveal my thoughts to my preschool daughter. She assures me she understands me.

When she was approaching her fourth birthday, she asked me if she would still get to keep her same letters when she turned four.

"Will I still be M-A-N-D-Y?"

"Yes, Mandy, you will."

She seemed satisfied with that answer, as if it were the last great answer to the mystery of turning four. We ask God questions like that as well and are just as sure we understand the mystery of life when we find answers to our questions.

He who forms the mountains, creates the wind, and reveals his thoughts to man, he who turns dawn to darkness, and treads the high places of the earth—the LORD God Almighty is his name.
                                                          AMOS 4:13

35

HIS THOUGHTS ARE HIGHER THAN MINE.

*H*ow much higher? Higher than mine are above my preschooler's, higher than the heavens are above the earth.

I suppose the more humble you are, the more you are able to grasp this thought.

As the heavens are higher than the earth,
so are my ways higher than your ways
and my thoughts than your thoughts.

ISAIAH 55:9

36

HE IS AWESOME.

*But just telling you
this isn't enough.
To understand,
you'd have to get to
know Him yourself.*

---

*Do not be terrified . . . for the LORD your God,
who is among you, is a great and awesome God.*
                    DEUTERONOMY 7:21

37

HE IS THE GOD OF SECOND CHANCES.

Starting Over

*S*tarting over. Sometimes I think I'm the queen of starting over, or at least the queen of making dumb mistakes that necessitate starting over. Like the time I was in the seventh-grade typing class. All the students in the room were learning to place their fingers in just the right position on the keys. I was so excited to be learning to type. For years I had looked in envy at others who made words appear at lightning speed. Back then, in the sixties, we didn't have computers in school; we had typewriters, and typing was the thing. So there I was, learning exactly what I'd dreamed of learning. Only there was a problem.

The whole class seemed to be taking too long. They were going so slowly. I wanted to speed things up. So I cheated. When the rest of the class was doing what the teacher said to do—looking at the paper, not looking at the keys—I looked at the keys. If I hadn't, I wouldn't have been able to finish first. And in those days, being first was far more important to me than being obedient.

As the weeks went on and everyone else was typing so slowly, I was smug in my ability to speed type (while constantly sneaking peeks at where each key was located).

Ha, I was the all-time winner—until one day I showed up for class and all the keys on the typewriter had been blacked out. Someone had covered up the keys, so we couldn't cheat even if we wanted to. For the rest of the class, this was no problem—they had been doing the right thing for weeks, and their efforts paid off. For me, it was disaster. My gig was up. I'd been cheating, and my sins were found out. I couldn't even type one sentence. I didn't know where any of the keys were. There was only one thing to do.

If I ever wanted to move forward, I had to go back and start over. So I did. I spent the next few weeks back at square one, going through the process that everyone else had already gone through. I typed for days, alone in a room, looking only at the paper, not at the keys—so that one day I could rejoin the class. I was embarrassed, but at least I was moving forward.

Now you'd think after an experience like that, from then on, I'd always do the right thing. But no. I'm still out to get around the rules. I can't tell you the number of times I've messed up, thinking it was better not to follow the rules only to have to pay the piper later.

Today, for example, I had to pay the piper. Only the piper was an orthodontist. My mouth was fitted for braces—a second time—less than a year after I got my braces off the first time. "Wear your retainer," they'd said. "If you don't, your teeth will move." I didn't see how my teeth could possibly move. I reasoned that I'd been in braces so long, if my teeth didn't know where to be by now, they'd never know. They were too straight to move. So for a variety of good reasons, all backed up by my own understanding, I didn't wear my retainer. Today, I had to get my teeth rebanded. They are a mess again. I had to pay big money *again*—money we hadn't counted on, money that could have gone toward replacing our sick car or paying bills accumulated in trying to fix our sick car. That same money could have been used to fix up our broken-down house or our broken-down furniture or a myriad of other things.

And don't even get me started on the time I didn't pay my taxes because I didn't have the money. I was single then, and it was only a few hundred dollars. The IRS would just take it out of my next year's refund. Right? Wrong. The IRS had far bigger things to worry about than me. Right? Wrong. The IRS would take down my new address off my next year's filing form and mail me a bill. Right? Wrong!

Eight years later and happily married, my husband and I received an enormous bill. The few hundred dollars had now become a bill with interest tacked on from day one, plus penalties and more interest on the penalties, and penalties for not paying the interest on the penalties. The bill was so big we didn't have enough money in savings to pay it. I watched sadly as my husband took out a loan to pay it. Will I ever learn—to obey, to do the right thing? I hope so. At least I'm learning that there is always another chance, while I'm alive, for me to start over.

I know there are tons of people in the Bible who made big mistakes and started over—Moses, David, Paul, Peter, and the man on the cross next to Jesus. The whole Gospel is predicated on the fact that no matter what you've done or how much you've done of it, you can start over. As long as there is at least one breath in your body and a desire to do the right thing, it is not ever too late.

Today, I don't look at the keys when I type. I pay my taxes on time. And I'm gonna wear my retainer when these new braces come off. And there are a million other lessons I've learned, but the big one I want to tell you today is that if you feel you're a bigger mess up than I am, cheer up! Jesus knows all about it. He already died on a cross for you, and He wants you to come to Him and live one day at a time, starting over each day, 365 days a year.

Besides, you know all those people who think they are so cool that they don't make dumb mistakes like I do and they don't need to start over? Well, they are the biggest fools of all. The Bible says all our self-righteousness is as filthy rags before a God who demands perfection. The good news is He has made provision for that perfection through faith in His Son.

He is the God of those who need such a big second chance that only being born again will work for them.

It is by grace you have been saved, through faith . . . not by works, so that no one can boast.
EPHESIANS 2:8-9

38

HE IS COMING BACK TO EARTH IN JUST A LITTLE WHILE.

*M*y daughter is four now and understands the concept of time much better than she did when she was three. But still, waiting is not something she does well.

"Mom," she says to me (several times an hour), "when will it be Christmas?"

"Soon," I say to her. "Soon."

The fact that time seems to pass much faster to me than it does to her doesn't mean that it actually does.

Similarly, even though it seems to me to be taking a long time for Jesus to return, God says it will happen in a little while.

In just a very little while, "He who is coming will come and will not delay."
HEBREWS 10:36

39

HE BRINGS OUT THE STARS ONE BY ONE AND CALLS THEM EACH BY NAME.

I don't understand a God like this, who brings out the stars one by one and names each one so He can actually call them by name and see them in their places. I don't understand a God like this, but it makes me love Him more.

Lift your eyes and look to the heavens: Who created all these? He who brings out the starry host one by one, and calls them each by name. Because of his great power and mighty strength, not one of them is missing.
ISAIAH 40:26

40

HE BLESSES THOSE WHO TAKE REFUGE IN HIM.

As if just the refuge weren't enough.

Blessed are all who take refuge in him.
PSALM 2:12

41

HE IS ON DUTY
24/7 . . .

. . . and all of the

long minutes in between.

Do you not know? Have you not heard?
The LORD is the everlasting God, the Creator of
the ends of the earth. He will not grow tired or
weary, and his understanding no one can fathom.
ISAIAH 40:28

42

HE HAS A GAG REFLEX.

Someone once told me the opposite of love isn't hate; it's indifference. And that is what makes God vomit.

So, because you are lukewarm—neither hot or cold—I am about to spit you out of my mouth.
REVELATION 3:16

43

DELIVERANCE COMES FROM HIM.

He may use time,
friends, parents,
training, education, or
your court-appointed attorney;
but still, the praise for the
deliverance belongs to Him.

From the LORD comes deliverance.

PSALM 3:8

44

HE RESTORES SOULS.

*S*ome people restore old cars. Some restore furniture. It's a wonderful thing to watch someone who loves the thing he is restoring set out to do his work. Sometimes a restoration takes years to complete.

I suppose God could use anything He wants to restore our souls—what is on earth or what is in Heaven. I like to think of Him that way—as the Great Restorer, painstakingly bringing back glory to a soul that has been tarnished by neglect or damaged from years of abuse.

He restores my soul.

PSALM 23:3

45

HE IS JEALOUS.

Not jealous of us
but for us.

Do not worship any other god, for the LORD,
whose name is Jealous, is a jealous God.

EXODUS 34:14

46

He never forsakes those who seek Him.

If you've ever been forsaken by those you have sought, you'll join me in appreciating this promise.

You, LORD, have never forsaken those who seek you.

PSALM 9:10

47

HE RENEWS STRENGTH.

*For those who wait on Him
with an active anticipation,
He will exchange His
strength for their weariness.*

---

*Those who hope in the LORD will renew
their strength. They will soar on wings
like eagles; they will run and not grow
weary, they will walk and not be faint.*
                                        ISAIAH 40:31

48

HE ENCOURAGES
THOSE WHO NEED
ENCOURAGEMENT.

Some of us need more

encouragement than others.

He knows that also.

You hear, O LORD, the desire of the afflicted;
you encourage them, and you listen to their cry.
PSALM 10:17

49

HE HELPS THOSE WHO CANNOT HELP THEMSELVES.

*W*hen I was growing up, a popular saying was "God helps those who help themselves." The only problem with that saying is that it suggests self-reliance, which the Bible says is not the way to Heaven.

In truth, God makes His help available to everyone, except those too proud to ask for it.

Trust in the LORD with all your heart and lean not on your own understanding; in all your ways acknowledge him, and he will make your paths straight. Do not be wise in your own eyes.
PROVERBS 3:5-7

50

HE DOES NOT WANT ANYONE TO PERISH.

I pray for my daughter. I want only the best for her; but she has her own will, and she's exercising it more every day. I don't want her to do things that have negative consequences, but if she does them, she does. I'd rather have her use her own will and face consequences from her choices than for me to turn her into some kind of a safe robot with no will, no choice.

God feels that way as well. He doesn't want anyone to make choices that have negative consequences, but He leaves the choice to us. He doesn't want a robot for a child any more than I do.

The Lord is not slow in keeping his promise,
as some understand slowness. He is patient
with you, not wanting anyone to perish,
but everyone to come to repentance.

2 PETER 3:9

51

THE HEAVENS DECLARE HIS GLORY, THE SKIES PROCLAIM THE WORK OF HIS HANDS.

*W*hen my husband was in college and was on one of his many backpacking trips, he looked around himself at the beauty of the world and its heavens and asked God, "If You're real, please bring someone to show me more of You."

My husband would tell you I was the answer to that prayer.

I think it's a good prayer for any seeker and any lover of outdoor beauty.

The heavens declare the glory of God;
the skies proclaim the work of his hands.
                                    PSALM 19:1

52

HE IS A FRIEND OF THE OPPRESSED, THE WEAK, AND THE NEEDY.

*S*ome people are so insecure, they don't like to be seen with anyone who isn't powerful. God isn't like that. He's not insecure at all and loves being a friend to those who are oppressed, weak, and needy.

You have been a refuge for the poor,
a refuge for the needy in his distress.

ISAIAH 25:4

53

HE GUARDS THE COURSE OF THE JUST AND PROTECTS THE WAY OF THOSE WHO FOLLOW HIM.

Just in Time

*G*od can use anyone or anything to accomplish His plans. He once used a common ass (see Numbers 22:28-30), so I shouldn't be shocked that He sometimes chooses to use me. In the fall of 1999, God used me to make two phone calls that helped guard and protect the publishing career of a young man I barely knew.

The man was Michael Morris. We were both attending the 1999 Maui Writers' Conference. Michael had written a novel about a woman who runs away from an abusive husband and ends up finding in unlikely places a friend and a faith. While in line for one of the seminars, Michael told me how he came to attend this particular conference that was so far from his North Carolina home.

"I prayed about it," he said, "and through different sources, the tickets came gratis; and then the lodging was free as well. I just took this to mean I was supposed to be here."

"No kidding, Michael? That's great! But, why didn't you bring your novel with you? Every agent here is asking to see it."

Michael couldn't answer that one. He was going to send the novel to everyone as soon as he got home.

Because we never had more than five minutes at a time to talk, Michael and his wife, Melanie, invited me out to dinner on the last day of the conference. But as my last meeting went late and I realized how exhausted I was, I called to cancel. I knew I'd never see Michael again, so I just committed him to the God who keeps what is committed to Him.

The next morning, I was running late. I had to clean up the room where I'd strewn clothes, books, and papers; and I was trying to figure out how I was going to return a rental car and still make my morning flight.

When all four of my bags were packed and by the door, I looked around the place one last time. At that moment in my heart, I heard a voice I've come to recognize as being from the one I serve saying, "Stop and call Michael Morris."

"Lord," I said, "I can't. I'll be late. I'll call him tomorrow morning when I'm home and not so hurried."

"Call him now." There was urgency in the command. I argued with God for a few minutes. First, who even knew whether this was the voice of God? Why would God want me to call Michael? I hardly knew Michael and really had nothing to say to him. Why couldn't a call like this wait?

But there is something that people who believe learn early in their walk of faith, and that is to trust and obey and not lean on their own understanding. So not knowing the outcome or why the sense of urgency, I set down my luggage and said, "Lord, if I do this, it's up to You to get me to the airport on time."

I phoned Michael Morris, and when he answered, I said, "Michael, I know this sounds strange, but the Lord just told me to call you and ask you to send me your manuscript, overnight express, as soon as you get home." (Sometimes when we act on faith, God puts words in our mouths.)

Michael said, "Okay." I kept repeating to him that he had to send his work to me as soon as he got home that evening. I told him I hadn't wanted to call him right then but had felt urgency from God. Then we hung up the phone and I called a cab (after the rental company agreed to pick up the car at the hotel, something they had never done before). I made my flight. I didn't think of Michael Morris again until his manuscript arrived the next morning.

I started reading his novel and knew instantly it was going to be a best-seller. I called the office of my new agent and reached his wife. "Susan," I began, "You have got to sign this guy. He is the greatest."

"Marsha," Susan said, "we're not taking new clients."

"Susan, this novel is wonderful. It's not all sweetsy weetsy; it's about real life. Then I told her about it in one breath and ended by saying, "Here, let me get Michael on the phone."

It crossed my mind while I was dialing the three-way call that Michael Morris and Susan Yates lived three thousand miles apart from each other. I wasn't sure how they would ever meet, but I didn't want to bring that up at the moment. I'd worry about it later.

"Susan, this is Michael. Michael, this is Susan."

We all talked for a few minutes—Michael explaining his novel and I raving about it. Then Susan said she had to run because she had to pick up tickets for a trip she and her husband were taking the next morning.

"Well," I said, "I would love for you guys to meet, but Michael lives far away. He lives in North Carolina."

There was a sudden dead silence from Susan. Then, seeming to catch her breath, she said, "You live in North Carolina?"

"Yes," said Michael.

"My husband and I are going to be in North Carolina tomorrow."

"You're kidding,.." I said.

"I'm not kidding," said Susan. "I'm going to pick up the tickets now. If you'd called just a few minutes later, you would have missed me. It's my first trip ever to North Carolina."

"You're kidding!" I said again. "You're going to be in North Carolina tomorrow?"

"Yep," she said. "Michael do you think we could meet for lunch?"

And that is how my agent met Michael Morris in North Carolina the day after she spoke with him on the phone—a phone call that was timed perfectly with a previous call in Maui, with an overnight delivery service, with tickets that had to be picked up within minutes.

God knows how to guard and protect the course of those who want to follow Him.

He guards the course of the just and
protects the way of his faithful ones.
PROVERBS 2:8

54

HE IS A KNITTER.

*M*andy asked me yesterday if God made Jay Leno. "Yes," I said. "When Jay Leno was a baby, God made him."

The Bible says God knits us together in our mothers' wombs. But one might say, "Surely He made a mistake with Mandy. I mean, He dropped a stitch when He allowed one of her genes to harbor the code for Celiac Disease. Either God is not good or He just wasn't looking during that part of her creation."

The answer to God's allowing Mandy to have Celiac Disease has to do with the fact that no one is created just for his or her immediate family.

We are all part of a greater-knitted quilt. The quilt includes the whole human race, both the physical and the spiritual aspects.

Mandy's intolerance to gluten has led me to campaign for a larger understanding of Celiacs and a greater awareness in those around me. And, I suppose, it has created a thankful heart in those who don't have to monitor every bite of food their children consume.

Each stitch God knits is important, not just for it alone but for what it supports in the greater scheme of things.

You knit me together in my mother's womb.

PSALM 139:13

HIS FAVOR SURROUNDS ME LIKE A SHIELD.

A shield is used for battle. This analogy implies we are in some kind of a moral or spiritual battle, and without His favor, we just aren't dressed to survive.

---

*Surely, O L*ORD*, you bless the righteous; you surround them with your favor as with a shield.*
PSALM 5:12

56

HE LOOKS DOWN FROM HEAVEN ON THE SONS OF MEN TO SEE IF THERE ARE ANY WHO UNDERSTAND.

*R*ecently my daughter, Mandy, asked me, "Momma, when I get older, will God be the boss of me?"

"He already is," I told her. "You just don't know it."

I suppose that sums up the state of the whole world—they just don't know or understand who is boss.

The LORD looks down from heaven on the sons of men to see if there are any who understand, any who seek God.

PSALM 14:2

HE BLESSES THOSE WHO DELIGHT IN HIS LAW.

*T*he odd thing is, He blesses them in two ways—by the delight they find in His law and by the result of obeying it.

Blessed is the man who does not walk in the counsel of the wicked or stand in the way of sinners or sit in the seat of mockers. But his delight is in the law of the LORD, and on his law he meditates day and night.

PSALM 1:1-2

58

THE EARTH IS HIS.

It is on loan to us.

The earth is the LORD's, and everything in it,
the world, and all who live in it.

PSALM 24:1

59

HE IS MY CAREGIVER.

God wants to be our caregiver, and His reputation and references are impeccable. His standards are so high, no one else's come close; and His motivation is love, pure love.

Cast all your anxiety on him because he cares for you.

1 PETER 5:7

HE WANTS TO COMFORT US IN OUR DISTRESS, SO THAT WE CAN COMFORT OTHERS WHO ARE IN ANY DISTRESS.

*M*y friend Susan is a part-time flight attendant who believes in staying in her Seattle-area home with her children. She doesn't fly much. She flies just enough to keep her benefits so her Mom, who lives in Atlanta, can fly out to visit her.

In September of 1994, Susan hadn't worked for fifteen months. She'd taken time off for the pregnancy and nursing of her second child, Jack. When Jack was five months old, Susan came back to work for just a few hours to keep her benefits current. She got on the plane and worked to SLC. When she landed, her husband phoned to say Jack had just died of SIDS,

Sudden Infant Death Syndrome. He had lain down for his morning nap and never woke up.

Susan didn't work again for five years. As word of her tragedy swept the bases of our company, everyone agreed—this is every mother's nightmare. Your first day back at work, your baby dies.

You would think that nothing good could come out of this. But amazingly, God has used this experience to give Susan an inroad to comfort other mothers whose children have died of SIDS.

Susan told me that nobody understands the SIDS experience like a mother who has been through it. These families will listen to her when they won't listen to anyone else.

We are all created not unto ourselves but to live in a great community of humans who have eternity written on their souls. Susan received comfort from the God of all comfort, and she has passed that comfort on.

Who comforts us in all our troubles, so that we can comfort those in any trouble with the comfort we ourselves have received from God.
2 CORINTHIANS 1:4

61

HE HOLDS VICTORY.

All victory for every
good thing is from
His storehouse, and
He is generous with it.

He holds victory in store for the upright.
PROVERBS 2:7

62

HE DISCIPLINES.

I don't like discipline; I never have. I don't like anyone telling me what to do or telling me I've done something wrong. (I'm just being honest here.)

But I like beautiful music, and the greatest music comes from disciplined performers.

And writing—I like the cadence of good writing. But writing is a discipline. For me, at least, it requires countless hours of practicing, working over and over until what is right flows from what was wrong.

And the game of beach volleyball—I love to watch it, but those players wouldn't be any good without discipline.

It seems there is a beauty that comes from discipline, or as the Bible calls it, "a harvest of righteousness and peace."

No discipline seems pleasant at the time,
but painful. Later on, however, it produces
a harvest of righteousness and peace.
HEBREWS 12:11

63

HE IS THE MAKER
OF GREAT MAPS.

He will show me

the path of life.

He will show me

where to find delight.

He will show me the

path to set my heart free.

I run in the path of your commands,
for you have set my heart free.

PSALM 119:32

64

HE IS LIVING WATER . . .

. . . to souls that are dying of dehydration.

Whoever believes in me, as the Scripture has said, streams of living water will flow from within him.

JOHN 7:38

65

HE IS THE GREAT PHYSICIAN AND WRITES THE SAME PRESCRIPTION OVER AND OVER AGAIN.

*H*e prescribes the Bible to be taken in on a regular basis. It is time-released. It is impossible to take too much of it. You must take it with an open heart for it to do any good. If you go a day without taking it, you may not feel weaker, but you will be.

Following this prescription will keep you healthier than you ever imagined.

All Scripture is God-breathed and is useful.
2 TIMOTHY 3:16

66

HE CAN USE CORRUPT LEADERS TO ACCOMPLISH HIS PLANS.

*O*ne of my favorite stories in the Bible is about Joseph. God allowed Joseph's corrupt brothers to wreck Joseph's future, or so they thought. If I were thrown into a pit and sold into slavery, I'd pretty much think my future was ruined. But not Joseph. He ended up becoming the second in command to one of Pharaoh's top officials because God gave him favor.

And after Joseph recovered from that betrayal, God allowed the words of one corrupt woman to have him thrown into jail—again, to ruin Joseph's life, one would think. If I had lost my job and my reputation and had been put into prison for years because of one false accusation, I'd think my life was ruined. But again, not Joseph. God gave him favor with the prison warden, who put Joseph in charge of all the inmates and all that went on there.

Through it all, God worked something in Joseph's life that could only be worked by suffering.

God can use corrupt leaders who bring suffering into our lives, but that suffering doesn't have to keep us down; it can be a learning experience. I don't understand it. I don't like it. But it's true.

Although he was a son, he learned obedience from what he suffered.
HEBREWS 5:8

67

HE KNOWS WHAT IT'S LIKE TO SWEAT OVER TEMPTATION.

*W*here was Christ when He came upon the greatest temptation of His life? Why, right in the center of God's will, of course.

Where was Christ when He came upon the second greatest temptation? Why, right in the center of God's will. In fact, where was Christ when He experienced every temptation known to man? He was exactly where God wanted Him. He was one with the Father.

The next time you're tempted, check to see where you are, and if you are close to the Father, take heart. He is with you always, even through blood, sweat, and tears.

His sweat was like drops of blood falling to the ground.

LUKE 22:44

68

IN THE BUNGEE JUMP OF LIFE, HE IS THE CORD THAT KEEPS ME FROM DISASTER.

*H*ave you ever watched someone bungee jump? The jumpers hardly pay attention to the secure, life-saving line until they are inches from disaster and it pulls them back from harm.

Sometimes we are like that with God, only noticing Him when disaster looms apparent.

They confronted me in the day of my disaster,
but the LORD was my support.

PSALM 18:18

69

He accepts those who are spiritually bankrupt and have no means of paying their debts.

I once had a warrant out for my arrest. I hadn't killed anyone. What I had done was simply treat the law as if it didn't apply to me. I had gotten fix-it tickets (fines for a broken tail light, blinker, that sort of thing) and one speeding ticket and had thrown them away. At the time, I didn't believe there was a place where they kept an account of such things or that a day of reckoning would ever come.

I was preparing the Sunday-school lesson for the next week's class when the warrant arrived. I called the police station to ask if it was for real.

"Oh yes," the operator said. "Quite real."

"Well, what happens now?"

"Well, when you have an outstanding warrant and you get stopped for any reason, they can haul you into jail."

"You have to be kidding," I said. "I'm not the jail type."

"That's what they all say."

I wanted to tell them all the good things I'd done in my life, but I realized that even if I told them every good thing about myself, it wasn't going to matter. I still had broken these laws, and they had it all on record. They didn't want to hear my protestations. I was someone who had committed infractions, and just like everyone else, I was going to have to pay.

Only, that was the problem. I couldn't pay. I was destitute, and they were asking for a hefty fine. But I certainly didn't want to go to jail.

"What does one do in this case?" I asked the police clerk.

"Well, you can appear in municipal court to appeal to the judge and see what he rules."

"What he rules?" *This is ridiculous,* I thought. *My fate is to be decided by one judge?*

I hated this. But just because you hate the thought of something doesn't mean it isn't real. I called to schedule a day in court, and I started to get scared. I decided to tell the judge the truth. I simply didn't have the money to pay the fine levied against me, and I just hadn't taken the law seriously. My appearance date was recorded in the books.

The judge sat so high up you couldn't see him unless you stood back a bit. A court reporter sat below, taking down every word being said. When it was my turn, they asked how I pleaded. I tried to explain I had a story to tell. They just kept trying to get me to say one or two words: "Guilty" or "Not guilty."

I finally said, "Guilty with an explanation." Then I told the judge what had happened, how I'd ignored the law and that I had no money now to pay the fine they were asking. "I need mercy," I said.

The judge looked at me, listened to me, and then slammed his gavel down and said in a loud voice, "Fine waived, exit right."

"But . . . ," I said, wanting to chat awhile, not understanding what was going on.

"Fine waived, exit right!" the judge yelled again.

"But . . . ," I said again, "what about the money?"

Then a uniformed policewoman came to me and took my arm and led me out of the courtroom as the judge yelled for the third time, "Fine waived, exit right!" The lady who was helping me out of the court explained to me that I didn't have to pay the fine that had been charged to me. I was free to go home. The judge had set me free.

Now, I know it's not correct to use this illustration with Christ because our fine wasn't waived, it was paid by God's Son. But still, I now know what it is to appear guilty before a judge who has the power to dole out a punishment that I never liked to think about.

And I also know the gratitude that washes over the one who was charged but then is set free to exit right, to go home.

The whole experience made me love even more the Great Judge, before whom we all will one day stand.

He brought me out into a spacious place;
he rescued me because he delighted in me.
PSALM 18:19

70

HE IS IN THE BUSINESS OF BUYING BACK WHAT WAS ONCE HIS.

*W*hen we were babies, we were all His. Then we got older and made choices of our own. We wandered away from what was written on our souls. Now He wants to bring us back. So He came down to where we live and entered the horrible pawnshop of this world. He walked up to where such things are decided and laid down His life to buy us back.

Now there is a way to freedom—but still, He leaves the choice to us. He is in the business of buying us back and loving us; He's not in the business of forcing us to receive that love.

The love is His. The choice is ours.

This is how we know what love is:
Jesus Christ laid down his life for us.
1 JOHN 3:16

71

HE IS IN THE PROCESS OF TURNING WHAT IS BITTER INTO WHAT IS SWEET.

I don't understand how He does it. Sometimes He uses time, and sometimes He uses friends. But I have seen Him, time and time again, take a bitter life experience and turn it into a sweet time of learning.

When they came to Marah, they could not drink its water because it was bitter. . . . So the people grumbled against Moses, saying, "What are we to drink?" Then Moses cried out to the LORD, and the LORD showed him a piece of wood. He threw it into the water, and the water became sweet.
EXODUS 15:23-25

72

HE IS INVISIBLE, YET HE MAKES HIMSELF KNOWN.

*M*y friend Janie used to have a picture frame hanging in her home—just the frame with no picture. There was an inscription on the bottom portion of the frame that read, "Though you have not seen Him, you love Him."

We worship a God who left us no record of His face yet has made Himself known through His Spirit and through His creation.

We can only see Him with the eyes of our spirits, which have the clearest vision of all.

Though you have not seen him, you love him;
and even though you do not see him now,
you believe in him and are filled with
an inexpressible and glorious joy.

1 PETER 1:8

73

HE IS TRUTH.

*M*aybe you are like Pilate and are standing right before Christ, asking Him, "What is truth?"

The answer requires a leap of faith that could be costly to one's upward mobility. Pilate didn't want to pay that cost or make that leap.

"What is truth?" Pilate asked.

JOHN 18:38

74

HIS EXISTENCE IS NOT VALIDATED BY MAN'S BELIEF.

*S*ome things are just true, like eight times eight equals sixty-four. If you believe it, you do; and if you don't believe it, you don't. But just because you don't believe it doesn't mean it isn't true.

He is before all things, and in him
all things hold together.

COLOSSIANS 1:17

75

HIS POWER IS MADE PERFECT IN MY WEAKNESS.

*M*y preschool-aged daughter, Mandy, will sometimes break a toy and then refuse my offers to fix it. "I'll do it myself!" she says, as she turns her back on me and tries to wrap up the mess she's made.

My strength has been offered and is readily available; but I won't intervene, because Mandy refuses my help. As long as she is claiming not to need me, she won't get me. I won't compete with her for control.

God is like that. He offers His strength to "fix what is broken," but as long as we insist on "doing it ourselves," He will leave us to our own devices.

However, He never stops listening to our hearts' cry, and the tiniest whimper of an "I am weak" prayer will be answered by His eternal strength.

My grace is sufficient for you, for
My strength is made perfect in weakness.
2 CORINTHIANS 12:9 NKJV

76

EVERYTHING MATTERS TO HIM.

*O*ne of the biggest lies of Satan is "It doesn't matter." Everything matters—eternally. There are no small sins, no tiny lies, no unnoticed slights.

Everything is huge in the kingdom of God but especially His grace, mercy, and peace.

Just as the result of one trespass was condemnation for all men, so also the result of one act of righteousness was justification that brings life for all men.
ROMANS 5:18

77

HIS LOVE
ENDURES FOREVER.

*W*hen my husband married me, he promised to love me forever, but I think the Lord had blinded his eyes (in sort of a reverse miracle). Or maybe he just didn't realize what awaited him.

He's spent the last fourteen years being made aware of things—like the way I keep a car. He loves a perfectly neat car, but he married someone who thinks of a car as a large piece of luggage in which to keep unfolded laundry, not to mention unwrapped food items and uncapped pens.

The truth is, I once left so much open food in the car that the whole thing became infested with ants. And another time, I accidentally spilled a glob of Milk Duds on the passenger seat. When my girlfriend saw the melted pile of brown gooey nuggets, she requested a butt mat.

So I pulled a towel from the pile of laundry in the backseat and laid it over the whole sticky mess. Then she sat on it and sort of flattened it.

I forgot to tell my husband why the towel was there, and the next day his boss unexpectedly asked for a short ride. Tom looked down at the towel and went to flip it off the seat. It was stuck to the seat. He lifted it up to look under it. Then he said, "Earl, would you mind riding in the back?"

Recently I asked Tom what went through his mind with that incident. He said, "Nothing printable."

I sometimes wonder, after fourteen years of continual experiences like this, if Tom would have made the same promise had he known my flaws up front, if the future had been played before him at the altar of his promise.

The thing about God is that the future *was* before Him at the altar of His promise. He already knew the horror of my sins (things greater than melted Milk Duds). He already knew all about my past and all the junk in my future, and still He has promised His love will endure forever.

That's God. He knows; He loves; and His love endures forever.

Give thanks to the God of heaven.
His love endures forever.

PSALM 136:26

78

HE HAS ONLY OUR GOOD IN MIND.

*W*hen my daughter, Mandy, is in trouble, she won't look me in the eye and she runs from my words. Although I have only Mandy's good in mind when I'm correcting her, she can't grasp that. She is so consumed with what she did, what she knows is wrong, that she wants to run away and hide.

It breaks my heart that I am like that with God, forgetting who He is and how He loves. I sin, and then my first instinct is to run and hide.

The LORD is slow to anger, abounding in love and forgiving sin and rebellion.
NUMBERS 14:18

79

HE FILLS OUR HEARTS WITH JOY.

C. S. Lewis said he was surprised by joy. I am overcome by it. And I've noticed my capacity for it can grow as I grow closer to God.

He . . . fills your hearts with joy.
ACTS 14:17

80

He understands.

*T*here is a chasm of difference between understanding and excusing. Our world forgets that, thinking instead that if you understand, you automatically excuse.

God understands every nuance of why we do every wrong we do. His compassions are new every morning. Yet He says we are without excuse.

Someone has to pay. Someone did pay. That Someone turned out to be God Himself in the form of a baby. This baby grew into a man who was truly innocent yet was sacrificed for the sins of many. Now the world can understand that there is a price paid for sins, even sins that are completely understandable.

He sacrificed for their sins once

for all when he offered himself.
HEBREWS 7:27

HIS CHARACTER
IS COMPLEX.

*I*f you were to ask the lady at the grocery store what I'm like, she'd tell you I'm always running around, planning good treats for my family.

If you were to ask Mandy's preschool teacher what I'm like, she'd tell you I'm a very protective mom.

If you were to ask the woman who was flirting with my husband at the restaurant last night, she'd tell you I'm not very warm to those I perceive as trying to steal my husband's affections.

If you were to ask my husband what I'm like, he'd tell you, "She's never boring."

If you were to ask the man who sat next to me on the plane last week, he'd tell you I was quiet, because I had my nose in a book the whole time and didn't say two words to him.

All these people would be right. These are all facets of who I am. God is like that too.

If you were to ask the children of Israel what He was like, they'd tell you He had a lot of rules and led them with a cloud.

If you were to ask believers in Christ what God is like, they would tell you all His rules can be summed up in one, "Love the Lord your God with all your heart, mind, and soul, and love your neighbor as yourself" (Mark 12:30).

If you were to ask Solomon what God is like, he would tell you that God dwelt in the "holy of holies."

If you were to ask the Jewish evangelical Paul, he would tell you, "God doesn't dwell in temples made by man."

All of these answers would be right.

Only those who get to know Him get to see His different facets. His complex personality, no one can figure out.

They do not know the thoughts of the LORD;
they do not understand his plan.

MICAH 4:12

82

HE LOVES MUSIC.

Many of us, when we
are happy, like to sing.
God shows His happiness
with us by singing.

He will rejoice over you with singing.
ZEPHANIAH 3:17

83

HE USES THE FOOLISH, WEAK, LOWLY, AND DESPISED SO THAT NO ONE MAY BOAST BEFORE HIM.

I have a friend who prides himself on being beyond cool—so cool he doesn't even need to use the word. You look at him and know he's cool. His parents are cool; his wife is cool; his clothing is cool; and his friends are cool.

He asked me once why there seem to be so many outcasts attracted to Christianity and in churches. "There are so many geeks there," he said, "so many misfits."

At first I wanted to argue with him and tell him of all the cool Christians I'd met—people who would leave him in the dust if there were some type of "really cool" competition. But then I thought about his question awhile, and I remembered this verse and realized he's right. There are a lot of misfits who are Christians.

Maybe God finds it easier to pour Himself into those who are emptied of self rather than being full of themselves.

That's the only answer I know.

Brothers, think of what you were when you were called. Not many of you were wise by human standards; not many were influential; not many were of noble birth. But God chose the foolish things . . . the weak things . . . the lowly things . . . the despised things . . . so that no one may boast before him.
1 CORINTHIANS 1:26-29

84

HE ONCE USED
AN ASS TO SPEAK
HIS WORDS.

And you thought

He couldn't use you?

The LORD caused the donkey to speak.
NUMBERS 22:28 NLT

85

HE HEALS.

I have seen Him heal hearts and change lives. I have seen Him take away grudges and misguided passions, make lame people walk and the blind to see. But don't just take my word for it; read the Bible and see for yourself.

---

*Everyone who asks receives;
he who seeks finds; and to him
who knocks, the door will be opened.*

MATTHEW 7:8

86

HE HAS REGARDED THE PRAYER OF THE DESTITUTE.

We are all destitute

in one way or another.

He will respond to the prayer of the destitute.

PSALM 102:17

HE SATISFIES.

I've often thought of the concept of consumption without satisfaction. I have had friends tell me that as alcoholics they were never satisfied, even when they passed out from too much of what they thought would satisfy.

Our world equates mass consumption of sex, food, drink, or shopping with mass satisfaction.

Yet, it doesn't work that way. In fact, consumption usually increases dissatisfaction. The only thing I've seen in my lifetime and in the lives of others that really satisfies is a relationship with God through Jesus Christ. I know that may sound strange, but it's true. And the really odd thing is, when one has his or her soul satisfied, enjoyment for all the other consumptive processes is enhanced. It's like if you seek first that one issue, all the other things will be added to you.

He satisfies the thirsty and fills the hungry with good things.

PSALM 107:9

88

HE SETS THE BARREN WOMAN IN A HAPPY HOME.

*I*n February 1996, I was reading an article of mine that had just come out in the *Christian Reader* magazine. The article was about the eight-year struggle my husband and I went through to have a baby but how we were finally told by specialists that we needed to accept the fact we would never have biological children. It told how we had been considered too old to adopt according to some agencies and too poor to afford the fees of other agencies. The article told how, through all this discouragement, I clung to the words of a friend of mine who said, "Marsha, somehow, I don't know how, but somehow, God is going to use your whole struggle with infertility for His glory."

I had been praying for months for a glimpse of that glory. Following is the story of what happened next.

Special Delivery

For six months, I'd been praying earnestly. I'd asked everyone I knew, and even some I didn't know at all, to pray that somehow, if it was God's will, my husband, Tom, and I would be able to have a baby.

The most precious prayers were offered by little children. One five-year-old prayer-warrior friend gave God suggestions. "Dear God, please send Marsha a baby. Maybe someone could give her one or she could just find one on the street. Thank you. Amen."

My husband didn't pray. He'd stopped praying after the last specialist told him all the reasons I'd never conceive. He'd stopped praying after the last adoption agency turned us down. He'd stopped praying after he realized the cost of a private adoption, and he'd stopped praying when he realized I was in full-blown menopause.

Being a scientist, Tom had seen all the facts. And in his lifetime, he'd never seen prayer change facts.

As I reread the *Christian Reader* article I'd written six months before, I suddenly didn't feel well. Something wasn't right.

Maybe you have cancer, the hypochondriac in me taunted.

I made an appointment with the infertility clinic. I told them my concerns and asked for tests—including one more pregnancy test. They looked at me with pity in their eyes and said gently but firmly, "No."

"The doctor has shown you your hormone count. You haven't had any cycles for seven months because you are in menopause. Asking for another pregnancy test only indicates you are not accepting things as they are." Although they didn't come out and say it, they implied I needed a therapist to help me deal with my infertility. I begged for the extra test; they resisted.

Finally, I convinced them. But they weren't going to rush the test through while I was there. Why bother?

The next day at home, the phone rang.

"Marsha, your pregnancy test came back positive."

"For what?" I asked. *Maybe there's some new type of cancer that only shows up on a positive pregnancy test,* I thought to myself.

"For pregnancy."

"What?"

After the sixth repetition, I said, "Could you hold for a minute? I'd like to get my husband on the phone."

With trembling fingers, I speed-dialed a three-way call.

"Tom," I said with urgency in my voice, "I've got the hospital on the line. Nurse, could you please tell my husband what you've just told me?"

"Your wife's pregnancy test came back positive."

"For what?" Tom also wondered if something was wrong.

"For pregnancy. Your wife is pregnant."

With characteristic understatement, Tom said, "Well, that's interesting."

The next day I went in for a sonogram. A heartbeat wasn't visible yet, but there was a yolk sac.

From a blood test, they determined I had conceived eleven days before. It was exactly the time for me to get supplemental progesterone to help the baby adhere to the uterine wall, which had been one of my problems in conceiving.

Over the next fourteen days, I had four more pregnancy tests and three more sonograms at the hospital's request. I think they were having trouble dealing with the facts.

The first time I saw the little heart beating, I burst into tears.

My full-term pregnancy was uneventful— unless you count every day bathed in praise for the answer to our prayers. On October 22, 1996, Amanda Joy was born. We call her Miracle Mandy.

It's hard to imagine a child who was ever more loved or such a great boost to her daddy's belief in prayer. In our kitchen by the back door, there's a little imprint of Amanda Joy's feet when she was just a few months old. Underneath the imprint is a verse: "What is impossible with man is possible with God."

We often tell our little prayer-warrior friend that God listened to and took a child's suggestion. We did find our baby on the street—the street of faith, paved by the prayers of believers.

He settles the barren woman in her home as a happy mother of children. Praise the LORD.
PSALM 113:9

89

HE IS SLOW
TO ANGER.

He does not have

a hot temper.

---

*The LORD is slow to anger, abounding
in love and forgiving sin and rebellion.*

NUMBERS 14:18

THE OUTCASTS OF SOCIETY ARE WELCOME AROUND HIM.

*T*his is a hallmark of divine love. When I am evaluating the impact of my life on earth, I ask myself, *Do the outcasts of society feel welcome around me?*

---

*This man welcomes sinners
and eats with them.*

LUKE 15:2

HE IS THE GREAT EXAMINER.

*T*here are two thoughts that come to mind here. First is the vision of an examiner from the IRS who has kept accounts and upon examination has found someone whose records render him prison material.

Second is the vision of a loving parent examining a precious child after a fall, looking for any problems or pains that require attention or comfort.

I suppose both interpretations of this verse could be true. It depends on whether you call God "Father" or not.

The LORD examines.

PSALM 11:5

92

HE IS THE KING OF GLORY AND THE PRINCE OF PEACE.

A king reigns.

A prince is an emissary.

Who is the King of glory? The LORD strong and mighty, the LORD mighty in battle.

PSALM 24:8

93

HE HAS COMMANDED US TO LOVE.

*G*od hasn't given us this command as an instructor would give a homework assignment, to be completed all by ourselves. Instead, this Instructor is right by our side, helping us on the hard parts.

Love one another.

JOHN 13:34

94

HIS LOVE CAN BE MADE COMPLETE IN US.

*This is the hope
of the world.*

---

*No one has ever seen God; but if we
love one another, God lives in us and
his love is made complete in us.*

1 JOHN 4:12

HE FORGIVES
THOSE WHO CONFESS.

C onfession is the key to forgiveness.

You might think that confession is a simple key. But truly, it can be a most difficult one because it involves humility, which is often more fun to observe than to practice.

He who conceals his sins does not prosper, but whoever confesses and renounces them finds mercy.

PROVERBS 28:13

96

HIS GLORY IS SO
TALL, NOBODY CAN
JUMP THAT HIGH.

We need someone

to lift us up—someone

whose reach extends

to Heaven.

---

*All have sinned and fall short of
the glory of God.*

ROMANS 3:23

HE LAUGHS.

*M*y daughter, who is under four feet tall and rather thin, swaggers up to me and says, "If any bad guys come, I'll just beat 'em up." And she's serious.

Her father and I look at her and laugh.

The Bible says God looks down from Heaven on the sons of men who conspire against Him, and He laughs.

The One enthroned in heaven laughs.

PSALM 2:4

HE WANTS US
TO BE CHILDLIKE.

The ones most mature

in the kingdom of God

are children at heart.

*I tell you the truth, anyone who will
not receive the kingdom of God
like a little child will never enter it.*

LUKE 18:17

99

THERE IS A MYSTERY TO HIS WHOLE PLAN.

While we may not understand all the clues along the way, He has already revealed the ending— He and His children win.

He made known to us the mystery.
EPHESIANS 1:9

100

HE IS NOT SURPRISED BY THE EVIL WE HAVE DONE.

I've heard people say, "Oh I couldn't tell God that. He'd be shocked at my behavior."

God is not shocked. He knows all and has seen all. In fact, when His Son died on the cross, all your evil was present and accounted for.

[Christ] bore the sin of many, and made intercession for the transgressors.

ISAIAH 53:12

101

HIS CHRISTMAS GIFT TO US COST SO MUCH, IT CAUSED THE ANGELS TO WONDER.

I was somewhere around thirteen years old and had long since stopped going to church. I didn't think God wanted to bother with a family like mine. My parents had been talking about a divorce. My stepdad was a pedophile and openly in love with our teenage baby-sitter. He had recently signed himself into a mental institution.

To say I was not happy would be an understatement. It was Christmas 1964, and I went for a walk down the main street of our tiny town.

In 1964, it was still legal to play the words to Christmas carols in public. So over the loudspeakers, I heard Christmas carols—all the verses, all the words. I heard "Joy to the World,"

"Hark! The Herald Angels Sing," and "God Rest Ye Merry Gentlemen." And I began to pay attention to them because they seemed to be telling a story. I didn't let on I was paying attention. I just kept walking and listening. What they said sounded too good to be true.

"Hark! The herald angels sing
'Glory to the newborn King.
Peace on earth and mercy mild,
God and sinners reconciled.'"

God and sinners reconciled? What a concept. What would God want with sinners? Why would He bother?

"Joy to the world.
The Lord is come.
Let earth receive her King."

What was the deal with the King? Some king was born, and the world was joyful about it. I could understand that. The world loved kings. *Hmm.*

"No more let sin and sorrows grow
Nor thorns infest the ground.
He comes to make
His blessings flow,
Far as the curse is found."

Far as the curse is found? I certainly felt the curse in my home. *Could it be possible,* I wondered for a minute, *that the great Christ really wanted to be where the curse is found?*

"Hail the Heaven-born Prince of Peace.
Hail the Son of righteousness.
Light and life to all He brings,
Risen with healing in His wings."

Healing? Only sick people need healing. Could Christ have come to a family as sick as mine? No, I don't think so. I'd never seen a family like mine in church when I attended there. Mostly I just saw people who gave the impression that all was well and who looked down on those who gave other impressions.

Still, it was intriguing, this message that seemed to come through in the carols. This story seemed too fantastic: *Some king is born who brings healing and goes to those who are cursed. I suppose if it were true, it would be cause for singing. It could even cause angels to sing, if there were such a thing.*

"Born to raise the sons of earth,
Born to give them second birth."

Maybe they needed second birth because they'd trashed the first one.

As I contemplated these things, I suddenly realized my soul was filled with hope—a soul I wasn't sure I had, a hope I didn't know existed. And a thing like joy, true joy in the midst of everything. A promise.

It would be years before I'd act on what I heard. But there in that small town in 1964, on that starry night, it was good to hear hope and to experience joy in the midst of a barnyard of despair.

It saddens me now that in these years we don't play the *words* to carols anymore in public places. We need to hear those words over and over, to be reminded of their deep truth. We need to listen to the story of a God who sent His Son as a common baby who grew to be a man who offers a chance to have new life.

I miss the public carols. I think they could make a difference. They did in my life.

To all who received him, to those who believed in his name, he gave the right to become children of God.

JOHN 1:12

ABOUT THE AUTHOR

Marsha Marks is an accomplished speaker and writer, blending humor and spiritual insights as she presents Christ so the world will listen.

Her articles and short stories have appeared in such publications as *Campus Life Magazine, Eternity, Moody Monthly, The Christian Reader,* and *Writer's Digest* magazine. She is in demand as a speaker for youth and women's conferences across the country.

She has been a flight attendant for a major airline since 1985 and delights in the opportunity to share God's love with people she would otherwise never meet.

Marsha lives in Georgia with her husband, Tom, and their daughter, Amanda Joy.

If you would like to schedule a speaking engagement or write the author, please address your correspondence to:

marshamarks@aol.com

Or visit her Web site:
marshamarks.com